My Heart Is an Open Book

A Poetry Collection

Elizabeth Maldonado

TRAFFORD
PUBLISHING™

ISBN: 978-1-4269-2339-5 (sc)

Library of Congress Control Number: 2011904835

Trafford rev. 03/30/2011

 www.trafford.com

North America & international
toll-free: 1 888 232 4444 (USA & Canada)
phone: 250 383 6864 ♦ fax: 812 355 4082

TABLE OF CONTENTS

Chapter 1
Looking for Love

Chapter 2
Being in Love

Chapter 3
Losing your Love

Miscellaneous Poems

TO ALL MY READERS

My heart is an open book
My heart has been through so much love, pain and deception
I wanted to write this book with my heart and creation
Because some of you out there have gone through something very similar
And the poems I have written will sound very familiar
My heart is an open book was inspired by friends, family and of course me
As you start to read it, you will see
That some of these poems will really hit home
And just so you all know, that you're not alone
My heart is an open book is my gift to all of you
To all the ones that have been in love but who also felt like singing the blues
I hope that some of these poems touch your heart like it did mine
And don't feel bad if all of a sudden you feel the need to cry
All the emotions will begin to flow and the poems will feel like your own
But remember this always, you are not alone!

DEDICATION

I will like to dedicate this book first of all to my kids, Desireé, Steven and Kayla. They have been my life and inspiration to go on and the ones who have been there for me through all the struggles and mistakes I have made in my life.
To my kids I love you with all my heart.

I would also like to dedicate this book to the men that have come and gone out of my life because if it wasn't for them I would have not had the inspiration to write these love poems.

I would like to thank all my friends for giving me the strength and support and for also lending me their ear when times were hard. I thank them for also sharing their love stories with me in order for me to write something for them.

ACKNOWLEDGEMENTS

I would like to acknowledge my son Steven for his creative touch in gathering the photos for some of one of my poems and also the book cover.

Chapter 1

Looking for Love

Alone on New Years

The New Year will soon be here,
And I don't want to shed another tear.
Another year has passed me by
I have no love in my life and often wonder why?

I hear messages from friends and family and it's not enough
I have no one there to hug
When will this end?
I feel so sad and my heart feels nothing but pain.

I try to go to sleep before the clock strikes twelve
laying in my bed all by myself
Wishing that this year to come will bring me happiness
Because I deserve to have the best

He will hold me tight in his arms with a passionate kiss
As we toast to another year
He says to me, this is to you and I my dear
And to a very Happy New Year!

Birds of a Feather

Two birds in search of their love
Where are they flying nobody knows
Gliding and flying is what they do best
To find the one that will be part of their nest

It's just part of nature to find your mate
Which it's something that humans can also relate
We search for that special someone to be in our lives
Soon to be married to either our husbands or wives

How do we know when we're truly in-love?
How do we know if the other person will fit like a glove?
We pick and chose and we end up making mistakes
What is it that makes us different from all the rest?

I want so much to find the one and be with him forever
I want to be like birds of the father that fly together
I want my life to be complete with my other half
Will I ever be happy like many others have?
Maybe never but I must have faith!

Finding your Heart

I'm sorry that you've been disappointed in the past
I don't blame you if you're heart is wrapped around a cast
Afraid of being hurt again must be always on your mind
I feel your pain and understand how you must feel all the time

I sometimes think about giving my heart and soul to someone new
But the chances I have given to other people has been just a few
Not because I can't love another person with all my heart
Simply because I been hurt way too many times and it's been hard

I wish that I could take away all the pain that you've been through
But I know it will take time and time is what I'll give to you
I will break the cast around your heart and help you love again
And I will not give up until your heart has healed from all the pain.

Impossibilities of Life

There's an attraction that I cannot hide,
I know it's impossible and I know the reason why.
You are a forbidden fruit that I cannot eat,
But I'm very fortunate that we were able to meet.
I'm sure you're very happy with your kids and wife,
Your wife is lucky to have a man like you in her life.
She's also very lucky to have you by her side,
I wished I had a man like you that I cannot hide.
I still will like to hang out with you and I promise not to mention this again
Not just because I'm attracted to you, is the reason why I want to be your friend.
But because you seem to be a sweet person and in my life I want you to stay,
And if you ever need someone to talk to, I'm just a phone call away.
Please don't take this the wrong way
I don't mean to harm you in any kind of way
But, if I'm stepping out of line
I'll simply turn around and just say goodbye!

Secret Feelings

You will never hear me say,
All the feelings I have for you, till this day.
I will keep them all inside with a lock and key,
You will not hear those feelings come out of me.

I wake up every morning thinking of you,
And often want to call you, just to see what's new.
But I know that someone next to you is sleeping,
All the reasons why I don't call & tell you what I'm thinking.

My feelings for you have grown stronger throughout the years,
I'm just happy to know that you'll always be near.
Even though I know another man has given you a life
Each time I see you, you will bring the sparkle in my eye.

I think you already know how I feel,
And the love I feel for you is real.
I know that you're happy with the man you have married
My feelings will be a secret and you don't need to worry.

Understanding

I know is hard to step away
Of past relationships and I understand
No matter what people do or say
I will stand by you, and hold your hand.

Past relationships are like ghost in your lives
That appear and disappear in different places
It may also be like a sharp knife
That will cut your heart in many pieces.

It's also hard when you're trying to start again
And the other person just won't go away
My time with you will never go in vain
Because if you want me. I will be here to stay.

Being Lonely

There are no words to describe,
The loneliness I feel inside.
Too many nights sleeping all alone,
With no one else but my own.

I need a love in my life,
Someone laying next to me at night.
There's such an emptiness in my heart,
I don't even know where to start.

I know there will come a day,
When the love of my life will say.
I love you with all my heart,
And you and I will never part.

Face Un-Known

I wait patiently for someone to be in my life
A life that has been empty for such a long time
I've searched and searched and always end up in the wrong place
Always trying to find the image of his face

I don't know how much longer I must wait
All I know is that I need to find my soul mate
That special someone who will be with me day and night
Someone who will hold me so tender yet so tight

A face un-known but I know it's out there
Where else can I search, If I have searched everywhere
Trying not to give up in search of the love of my life
I know one day he will find me and ask me to be his wife

He will then whisper softly in my ear
You will never have to worry because I will always be near
I will love you forever. Day, night and year after year
I will make you so happy my friend, my lover, my queen.

Half Full

Some people look at a glass and say it's half full
Some people look at the same glass and say is half empty
If you compare that to your life and say is half empty then you're fool
Because a glass half full has more power in every way

In a relationship no one is perfect
But I believe that there has to be someone perfect for you
I have treated everyone with consideration and respect
My relationships have always ended and then I start dating someone new

I want my glass to be half full
I want my life to be with someone but I must be very carful
Not to end up thinking that my glass is half empty
It will be the end of my life and that's not my destiny

My glass will soon be half full
If not with you with someone new
I will not give up on love, I know it's out there for me to take
I just have to recognize my past relationships were simple mistakes.

Lonely Streets

I have walked on these lonely streets feeling lost
And sometimes I really don't know if I walked the same street
I have tried to find the hope of being with someone at any cost
I am so alone and lost
When will I ever find the man I am supposed to meet?
The man who will make all my dreams come alive
My other half, the other side of me who's everything I am not
I am tired of walking these lonely streets with no one by my side
I miss the touch of a man's arms around me, I miss that a lot
Where is he? I am so tired of dating!
Lonely streets I am tired of waiting!
I have turned corners and then realized I turned into a dead end
No one was there waiting for me
I turned around to walk another mile and there it was again
I have walked into another lonely dead end
Why does this always happen to me?
Lonely streets, my heart has been broken so many times can't you see!
I will continue to walk these lonely streets
I will not give up because I know he's out there waiting for me
At any moment I could run into him
Waiting impatiently with his arms open to see me walking and getting near
Even if I have to walk the entire world today and tomorrow
I will not let these lonely streets drown me in my own sorrow.

To Find the One

Timid words and sexy dimples on his face
Cruel memories so hard to erase
Trying so hard to pick up and make a new start
But the memories will be so hard to tear apart

Yet he goes on day in and day out
To walk around in this cruel world we all know about
Life always brings us ups and downs
To play with our lives like puppets and laugh at us like a bunch of clowns

He still believes in love and happy endings
Looks back and sees his life where he is standing
He knows that one day he will really find the one
Now isn't that what every person wants?

To find the one who will love you again and again
To find the one who will care for you just the same
To find the one who will hold you in their arms and not pretend
To find the one that will make you happy in the end.

First Date

Why is it, that on the first date everything feels so warm inside?
His touch and everything about him it's just hard to describe
The way he looks at you makes time go by so fast
But you know that night will end soon and it will be a thing of the past
How do you capture those special moments again?
How do you know if he's a good man?
How do you know if this is the one for you?
How do you keep it together so that you feel like everything is new?
First dates are very special and fun
But sometimes it all changes after it's all said and done
No matter how much you try to go back to that moment,
It's just not there anymore
That first date, the first kiss, your first touch
has now come and gone out the door.

10/7/09

Relationships

Why is it so hard for someone to make it work in a relationship?
Is it because we move on too fast and we don't start with friendship!
I'm tired of devoting myself and giving my all to one person
I'm tired of mistake after mistake for no reason
Have I run out of chances with all the men I've dated in the past?
Do we only get a few chances and that's why my relationships don't last?
I would like someone to tell me listen there's no one out there for you!
It would definitely hurt but I wouldn't waste my time trying to find someone new!
Relationships are hard and they're always so much pain at the end
Is like trying to bend a metal with your bare hand
There's always one person in the relationship that doesn't understand
Understand your feelings, your character or maybe they just don't give a damn!
I would like to know the secret that some couples have
How do they cope with all of the everyday issues that they share?
It can't be just love, trust, communication and sex appeal
I know I tried all that with my past relationships but none of it felt real.
Relationships are hard that's all I have to say
Maybe I have not found my true love and maybe it will be here one day
All I know is that I am done trying to force it to come to me
This next person will just have to see all that I could be!

10/2/09

My Twin

My twin is the other half that's missing in my life
The one who feels my pain and when I hurt he cries
The one who cools me off with his body because I'm hot
And the only one that could read each and every thought

It's an amazing thing when you have two people that fit together
It's like walking in the rain on a stormy day and you don't even mind the weather
It's like building a puzzle and you just can't find the last piece
And when you find it, you feel that sense of joy and relief

One day I will find my twin like that missing piece in the puzzle
We will live happily ever after like a romantic novel
We will hold hands even when we're grey and old
And the puzzle will be complete with two people very much in-love.

I wish for Love

I wish for love and found them in all the wrong places
I wish for love but found it in all the wrong faces
Too much confusion and too many mistakes
It's just so hard for one person to take
I wish I could find my other half that special love for me
I tried just about everything, where could it be?
That love that makes my soul glow
That grabs me by surprise, but also gentle and slow
That inconvenient love, strong nothing could break it kind of love
That when you look at me everything seems to disappear and is you and I alone
I wish for love but I'm weak now and I don't have the strength anymore
My heart has been kicked around and sometimes ended up on the floor
My heart is slowly dying in the loneliness of the one who will complete me
My heart can't take any more pain if it's not out there for me
I wish for love but I don't know where to look anymore
I wish for that one love that I could care for and completely adore
I wish for that special love who also feels the same kind of love for me too
I wish for love and I tried to find it but now I just don't have a clue

01/05/10

Wondering Thoughts

I wish I could get inside your head
To see my future and what lies ahead
I sometimes wonder where I will be
And if you can ever give me what I need

My wondering thoughts are killing me
My wondering thoughts can't make me see
The kind of person you really are
My wondering thoughts are tearing my heart

I lay my head down on my pillow
Hopping that my wondering thoughts would leave tomorrow
But then I wake up in the middle of the night
Holding my pillow really tight

Why can't I see what you feel for me?
Why can't I see what my future will be?
I want to spend my life with you
But my wondering thoughts just seem so true.

4/19/09

Two Souls One Body

Sometimes I dream that my soul escapes from my body at night
In search of my soul mate wondering the streets till the morning light
In search of that lost soul who has not found me yet
In search of the love of my life who's out there but I have not met
One day our two souls will come together and we'll become one
One day our two souls will unite and we will have so much fun
Loving and caring for one another till death do us part
No one will ever tear us apart!
I wake up in the morning from that wonderful dream
But no one is there laying next to me
Sometime I wonder if my dream will ever come true
But all I could do is dream and wait for you
Two souls one body is what I been waiting for
Two souls one body is what I'm searching for
My true love, my other half and my soul mate
The one who understands me, the one I could truly relate
The love I've been yearning for all my life
The one who will ask me to be his wife

2/2/10

Chapter 2

Being in Love

The First I Love You

The first time you said "I love you" to me
Was the day you truly made me see
How wonderful my life could be
To have your love and to always have you near
The first time I heard you say "I love you" out loud
I felt like floating to the clouds
To capture the moment and hear you one more time
The words I love you echoed in my mind
Time and time again I waited for those words from you
Time and time again I wanted to say "I love you"
Time and time again I kind of knew
That one day you would say those gentle words
"I love you"

01/28/10

A New Start

I looked outside my window this morning
The birds are starting to sing
The leaves on the trees are turning green
I finally hear and see that we are now in spring
The beginning of everything new comes in spring
Just like the love between us has a new meaning
A meaning of commitment and trust that no one can brake
We both know in our hearts that our love is not a mistake
We argue, we fight but we always forgive each other and make a new start
Because the feelings we feel for one another cannot tear us apart
Because we both know we belong together
A new start, a new beginning, it's all just like the weather
Winter, Spring, Summer and Fall
Season and changes we must go through it all
Adjusting to weather will keep us dry and warm
Even when we go through a cold winter storm
Love, Passion and Anger are just like the seasons
Adjusting to your partner and avoiding fighting for no reason
Getting to know the one we love it's just the same
That's what will keep us together in the end

Getting Back Together Again

The night we got back together
There were no questions to answer from one another
There were no explanations to our actions
It was just you and I holding each other tight
Your hands felt like fire on my skin
Wondering all the time where you had been
Your lips touching mine
Thinking why do we continue to fight all the time
I missed you so much and don't want to lose you again
I hope now you understand my pain
My pain of living without you
My pain of not being near you
Every time you touch me I feel like melting butter
Every time you kiss me, it feels like no other
Every kiss you give me has a different signature
That makes my body go through a low and high temperature
I love you with all my heart
I can't bared the thought of ever being apart
Getting back together again with you
Makes me feel special and new
Getting back together again, was always my plan
Because being apart from you, was nothing but pain.

Beat of my Heart

In every beat of my heart, I feel you
In every beat of my heart, I can hear you
Whenever my heart skips a beat
It's because it yearns for your body heat

Whenever your lips touch my lips it feels tender and sweet
Two bodies, two souls and one heart beat
Electrifying chills running down my spine
That's how the sound of my heart sends signals to my mind

Your hands caressing every inch of me
And down deep you know you hold the only key
The key that has the power to turn it on and off
Because you give me strength and know each and every thought

My heart is yours forever
My heart knows we will always be together
This heart beat controls the music in every tune
Just like the night needs the moon.

Lost in Lust

Seating on the porch on a beautiful night
Looking at the sky and counting all the stars
Thinking of your lips, your body and you holding me tight
Your skin so smooth, your tender kisses and feeling you so close but yet so far
Like looking at the sunset from an ocean view
Feeling the heat penetrate our skin
And drips of sweat that covers our bodies all the way through
The smell of passion all around the sheets where our bodies have been
My heat, your heat clashing together like ocean waves
Every motion of our bodies is like a melody that never ends
Locked in a room with no place to go like two slaves
Heavy breathing dries our mouth like desert sand
Together we embrace one another covered in sweat
With lust in our eyes like when we first met
All I see is you and I exhausted and wet
The rain has stopped, all I see is a rainbow and a beautiful sunset.

Our World to Own

If you came to me one day and said
You will be happy for the rest of your days
I would say you cannot be serious
But tell me because now I am curious

He then takes my hand
And into his pocket he reaches in
To take out a silver box
And in that box he opens up, there's a diamond ring

I will make you so happy my love
I will give you the world to own
I will give you the stars and the moon
This I will promise to you very soon

I look down to him as he is on his knees
Promising me the world and all that I need
As the tears in my eyes start to run down my face
With a smile on my face I answer I do
I will marry you

I will make you so happy my love
I will share with you my world you gave me to own
I will share all the stars and the moon
All of this I will share it with you very soon.

Reasons why

Reasons why people fall in-love are now too rare
Reasons why people fall apart just makes me sad
Two people who truly love each other should not go through pain
Against all odds, against the world proving their love is not in vain

I will fight for you my love. I will fight for you my friend
I will fight and fight the feelings that you and I have
No woman, no man will ever challenge the love that you and I share
No woman, no man will destroy us, this I will swear
For you are mine and I am yours till the end!

Reasons why some couples stay together and others fall apart
The reason is because some love with their mind and some love with their heart
You and I must love each other with our heart and soul
Reasons why we'll stay together now and forever more

I will have your back and you will have mine no matter what anyone says
Because the trust is there when I can look into your eyes and you look into mine
Because we both share a secret that few others cannot find
Reasons why two people fall in-love is you and I combined
I love you Sweet heart of mine my one and only true Valentine!

Thinking of You

When I close my eyes I notice a shadow in my mind
And what I see is the image of your body next to mine
An image I cannot erase because I am thinking of you
And at that moment I am wishing you're thinking of me too

Each time I'm with you and your body is touching mine
I feel warmth in my heart and chills down my spine
I feel complete with you and I know the reason why
Because I am so in-love with you and that's no lie

I yearn for you touch, your kiss and your body
I enjoy looking at you because I think you are so sexy
You turn me on so much and it's so hard to explain
But I will spend the rest of my life showing you time and time again.

Too Much Too Soon

When do we say it's too much too soon?
How do we know when we're both in tune?
Do we imagine all of our actions and feelings we have?
Or are we so desperate to find the love and we just don't really care!

Why do we push someone too much and too soon?
Is it because we yearn for love and we don't want to be alone?
Why do we care if we're with someone or not?
Because of Adam and Eve, that's what this is about!

Two people joined together through thick and thin
Two people as a couple and no one else in between
Two people loving each other for better or for worst
Two people embracing each other is what I love the most

We could never say that too much is too soon!
Everyone is different, who are we to judge their move!
Too much and too soon is love at first sight
Too much and too soon is you my darling and me by your side.

Valentine's Day

I would run a thousand miles,
Just to see your smile.
If a genie granted me a wish,
I would choose your kiss.

My love is deeper than the ocean,
I will never play with your emotions.
It is also stronger than steel,
And I will never stop telling you how I feel.

Day by day I count the seconds till I see you again.
Life for me will never be the same.
Ever since we met, you have put a smile on my face,
And ever since that day, it has been a
Happy Valentine's Day.

When I met you

I met a man who has been hurt in similar ways
I met a man who has experienced my kind of pain
I met a man who understands on how I feel deep inside
I met a man who makes me feel so good and that I cannot deny

This man is gentle and loving with a big heart
This man will go to the top of the mountain and back for you, he's just a work of art
This man is beautiful from the inside and out
This man could love someone so deeply without a doubt

I wish that one day I could be that special someone
I would love to be the love of his life and that's just for certain
To hold him and love him the way he deserves to be loved with no regrets
For better, for worst we could build our own little nest.

You are my Sun

You're like the sun that keeps me warm
You're like the sun that stops the winter storm
You're like the sun that wakes me up each day
And like the sun that stops the sky from turning grey

I see the sun up in the sky
And I don't feel the need to cry
The reason is because I am with you
You make everything also new

The stormy days have ended now
And all I have to say is Wow!
You are my sun that shines so bright
I want you always by my side

My life with you

Last night you brought me back to our first day
Like the first night we spent together and I didn't know what to say
You held me and touched me like it was the first time
You kissed my lips with such passion and I was back on your mind
We went back to the past and I felt wanted again
You caressed my body making love to me with sweet and tender pain
The kind of pain that two lovers yarn for and cannot be shared
To hold one another with desperation and aguish beyond compare
We made love time and time again till the morning light
It was so hard for us to even say good night!
After all the passion that we shared we held each other tight!
And even though we were tired we touch our bodies the entire night
My love for you is everlasting pure and very real
Because you're always on my mind and can't stop telling you how I feel
Sometimes I can't wait to get home so I can see your face
To tell you that my life with you is the only one I would like to embrace.
To tell you that my life with you is worth the risk to take
To tell you that my life with you is the only choice I want to make

10/29/09
11:25am

My Reflection in your Eyes

My mind wondered off last night to the time when we were in love
My mind wonders if our love is worth fighting for
I realize I no longer saw my reflection in your eyes
I also no longer want to hear all your lies
I remember when our love was once wonderful and I thought it was hard to break
But in reality I recognize we both made a lot of mistakes
Tell me! When did our smiles begin to fade?
And why do I feel so betrayed!
Tell me!, how do we go back and start all over again?
I'm just so afraid to lose you and afraid of all this pain
How do I go back to see my reflection in your eyes?
Because we need to do this soon before our love completely dies
I know that if we both have a small flame left in us
We can make it work if we both have trust
We can then see the reflection back on each other's eyes
And we will love each other for the rest of our lives

11/3/09
4:03pm

Opposites Attract

I have met the love of my life and I am so much in love
My heart beats a thousand times and I feel it down to my soul
Touching him and looking at him it's so hard resist
I never thought that a love like this could ever exist
The funny part of this love of mine is that I am like salt and he is like pepper
Both of us combined give flavor to the food to taste a little better
I am like a flower and he is like the soil
The flower cannot grow strong without the soil
He's like the sun and I am like the moon
This love we have for each other is everlasting and will not die soon
It's true when they say opposites attract
It's not just a myth but a true fact
We are so different you and I
We may never see eye to eye
And we both have our moments where we bump heads
But we always end up forgiving each other and it's just a thing of the past
There's never a dull moment with you because you put a smile on my face
You make me laugh when I am sad and blue
How you captured my heart, I haven't got a clue
I just want to tell you that my heart belongs to you
My love for you will always be true.

Searching no Longer

Searching for the one who's right for me
But couldn't find the one to be
My lonely heart
Piece by piece being torn apart
Now that I've met you
I will never again be blue
Seeing the lust in our eyes
Making me forget the hurt I've felt from other guys
Anywhere I'm at, my mind wonders off and thinks of you
Wondering if you will ever come to love me and if your love will always be true
This poem is the best I can do
To let you know how much I care for you
Not needing to search for that someone special
Realizing that my love for you is unconditional
I will love you forever
I won't break your heart ever
For years, not knowing where to go or where to turn to
So confused and not knowing what to do
Now that I've found that special someone
My searching is finally done
Searching no longer
My love for you will grow stronger
My last words are: I love you
And I'll always be true to you

Trust

How do I mend a broken heart?
How do I attach all the pieces that have been torn apart?
Patience, love and affection is always a start
I'll do whatever it takes but you also have to do your part
I know you don't trust anyone anymore
I also know that this is not your fault
Someone hurt you very bad in the past
And that's the reason why you are so sad
You have not used your heart since then
And I know you're afraid to use it again
But don't you worry because I'll be there to hold your hand
And show you that it's alright to trust once again.

We Belong Together

You may be thinking that we're going through some bad weather
But I know deep inside my soul that we do belong together
I can deal with the rain, the thunder and all the lightning in the sky
What I can't deal is for you not to be by my side
We belong together and sometimes we may not hear the same tune
We belong together because that melody will make sense very soon
We belong together please don't give up on us
We belong together and one day you will realize
Maybe we can't always get along
But the love we have for each other is very strong
We can get though the bad times if you just let it be
You will never be happy because you belong to me
There's no point fighting the emotions we have for one another
There's no reason why we shouldn't be together
Listen to your heart and everything will soon be clear
Because your heart and mine have the same beat

8/6/09

Fight to make up

We fight and sometimes we don't know the reasons why
We fight to get our feelings hurt until one of us says goodbye
Why do we fight so much if we both know we can't live without each other?
You know it doesn't bring us closer to one another!
I love you so much but can't find the way to get my point across
I tell you time and time again but it seems like you have a hearing loss
We fight to make up time and time again and you know that's insane!
I sometimes feel like there's got to be something wrong with our brain
Why do we fight to make up the following day?
Why do we fight to make up if we both know this is where we want to stay?
No matter what you do or say I know you will be back the next day!
No matter what I do or say you know we'll be together till we turn grey!
We love each other so much and we always miss each other's touch
We spend days without talking but we know we're each other's crutch
Fight to make up, what is this about?
Fight to make up, we are not children and we should grow up!
I 'm tired and I just don't feel like going through another break up!
I just want to be with you let's not fight anymore, can we just make up?

10/29/09
10:02am

Thinking of You

When I close my eyes I notice a shadow in my mind
And what I see is the image of your body next to mine
An image I cannot erase because I am thinking of you
And at that moment I am wishing you're thinking of me too

Thinking of you is all I do
Thinking of you, I will be here for you
Thinking and thinking is all I can do
Wondering if you're thinking of me too!

Each time I'm with you and your body is touching mine
I feel warmth in my heart and chills down my spine
I feel complete with you and I know the reason why
Because I am so in-love with you and that's no lie

I yearn for you touch, your kiss and your body
I enjoy looking at you because I think you are so sexy
You turn me on so much and it's so hard to explain
But I will spend the rest of my life showing you time and time again.

My Promise to You

When I look into your eyes
I see the both of us
When I see your smile
It all makes it worth while
On this day we take a journey to the rest of our lives
Just you and I side by side
With one foot in front of the other
There's you my love in my life forever
When you hold my hand I feel secure
When you hold me in your arms I feel your love is pure
We are different you and I my love
But that's exactly what makes us whole
I will love you
I will support you
I will follow you where ever you may lead me
Because I trust you
Because I belong to you and with you
And because you belong to me and with me
Today, tomorrow and through eternity
You are the love of my life
And on this day I become your wife
My promise to you here and on this day
Is all that I have and all that I am

1/29/10

On this Day

On this day I give myself to you
On this day I say the words "I do"
On this day I give you my heart and soul
And on this day you and I become whole
In front of all these witnesses, I promise to love you forever
I promise I will not hurt you ever
I thank the lord for bringing you to me
Because on this day you and I become we
You are now my present and my future
And together our lives will turn into an adventure
You are now the only man in my life
I am now the woman that has become your wife
I am now and will always be by your side
On this day I will wear this ring with pride
This ring represents my heart
Wear it, protect it, and never let out of your sight
Because I promise to always follow you in the dark or in the light
I'm yours forever
You're mine forever
Us together forever

3/29/09

Chapter 3

Losing your Love

Missing You

I miss the feeling of your touch
I miss your kisses very much
Sometimes I close my eyes and see your face
And it's your lips I'd like to taste
I want to hold you in my arms again
Today, tomorrow, each and every day
I never wanted to let you go
You are the person that I love
I think about you all the time
I cannot get you off my mind
I miss you sweetie oh so much!
This is all so painful and so hard
I wish this pain would go away
I cannot deal with it another day!
I try and try to get you off my mind
But all it does is make me cry
Cry because I couldn't make you love me like I do
Cry because I couldn't get through to you
I miss you now and I always will
Because my love for you was very real!

10/8/09

A Broken Heart

How does someone mend a broken heart?
How does someone raise a child with both parents apart?
I tried my best but for you it was never good enough
Now I see my child as much as possible,
but when she leaves it's always rough
Where did I go wrong, if I gave it my all?
Where did I go wrong, when we were so in love?
You never once understood where I was coming from
You just took my child from what could have been a happy home
I never want to go through this again
A broken heart like this, is heard to mend
Will I ever take this chance with someone else?
Will I ever have a happy family, no one can tell
I feel now like my manhood was ripped apart
And all I have to show for it, is a broken heart
My child is the only thing that keeps me alive
She's now my everything, she's my world, she's my whole life!

Heartless

I can't find myself anymore
You continue to hurt me and now my heart it's soar
I tried to be your friend
And yet you brought me nothing but pain

How could I make you understand!
That what you're doing must come to an end
How could I open your eyes!
So you could see the nights I have cried

How could you be so heartless!
When all I have tried to show you was kindness
Please just let me go
Have some compassion on this poor soul

I don't like the darkness I am in
I don't want to feel any more pain
Just do me a favor and be Heartless one last time
So the sun can shine on me and I can live my life.

I'm Sorry

I know I have destroyed what we could've been
I know it's too late to say, let us begin
I realize I was selfish and I couldn't see
What you really meant to me

You have been through so much in your life
But you have to understand that so have I
I'm sorry if I was not understanding to your needs
I'm sorry and I'm asking you down on my knees

I care about you more than you could ever imagine
I made a mistake but I guess I'm only human
Now I have to pay for this mistake
I just wish you can forgive me and still be my friend

I'm sorry, that's all I can say
I know that out of your life you want me to stay
I will not attempt another time, this is the last
Illusions of you will stay in my past.

12/21/2008

No answers to Why

Many nights I lay down and you were on my mind.
Thinking of you and wondering why?
Wondering why my life has been empty without you,
Wondering if God will ever send me a sign.

Why weren't you there to keep me warm?
Why is my heart still hurting inside?
Why couldn't you see all the love I felt for you?
Why did you have to leave me all alone?

You were the one I would give my life for.
You were the one that I thought of when I laid down at night.
You were the one that brightened my lucky star.
You were the one worth fighting for.

My nights of wondering "why" must come to an end.
If not tomorrow perhaps the next day,
And although, the next day may never come.
My nights of wondering "why" will remain in my head.

The Day we Said Good Bye

It all started with promises and words that had no meaning
The day we said good bye was the day my phone kept ringing and ringing
That day I had no words to express all the emotions I was feeling
I stood there looking at the phone while I saw all the calls I was missing
This behavior you mastered though out the time we were together
Making every excuse possible and me wishing it would soon be over
But it just got to be too much for me and I just stopped caring
That's why the day we said good bye had no effect on me and no meaning
Just like your words to me at the end of that last message
I don't know how after all the love I had for you I found the courage
The courage to let go and not look back at anything I once felt for you
I feel free and vision my life ahead, I can honestly see everything clear and new
I have no regrets, I feel no pain and I feel no more love for you
When before I felt like my heart was being torn apart because of you
We were not meant to be together and now I can clearly see that
Look at the picture and the memories we have left in the past
Nothing but emptiness and disappointments of you and I
Simply because we could never agree or see eye to eye
That's the reason why we came to this day and said good bye.

4/2/09

You're Hurting Me

I sit at night wondering, what am I doing?
Why do I love you so much when I'm just simply hurting!
Hurting from lack of communication and neglect
I thought you really cared and this relationship was so damn perfect!

I am not a part of your life and I have a feeling I will never be
This is not a real relationship and everyone can clearly see
I tried to be understanding but that didn't help at all
I tried to be compassionate and loving but you just ignore all my calls

You're hurting me, can you see how much I love you!
You're hurting me, can you see I will never hurt you!
You're hurting me, don't you understand what you're doing to me!
I'm tired of hurting and don't want to be with you if this is how is going to be!
Because you're hurting me!

I expected honesty, a loving relationship but I guess this is a hard task
I thought it was simple but I guess it's too much to ask
I don't like to feel like I am walking on egg shells with you all the time
I wish I could stop loving you and get you off my mind
But, I can't, you are just too deep inside, so what's it gonna be?
Because you're hurting me!

Take this Heart of Mine

I'm sitting in my bedroom
Just staring at the wall
Wondering if you will ever call
I am so all alone
Tell me now where did I go wrong
Tell me now where do I belong

My heart has been broken in a million pieces
I cry and cry just trying to drown your voice
Your voice telling me you would never hurt me
Your voice telling me you would never leave me

Take this heart of mine what do I need it for
Take this heart of mine, I don't need it anymore
Take this heart of mine, since I don't have you,
Just take this heart, I don't want it anymore
It hurts too much to have this heart now that you are gone

I used to lay next to you at night,
Feeling your arms around me holding me tight
But one day I woke up and you were no longer there
I was no longer in the reflection of your eyes
I was no longer by your side

You didn't even bother to say good bye to me
You just walked away without a word
Without an explanation of your actions
Silence is what you gave to me love is what I gave to you.

Un-Returned Love

Why do I love you so much?
Can't you see that my heart is crushed?
Can't you see the tears in my eyes?
I'd like to know why you're as cold as ice?

Maybe you're not meant to love anyone,
Maybe I will never be the one.
Maybe you can't see the pain I'm going through,
Maybe you will never say the words "I do"

I fell in love with someone that doesn't love me,
I don't think that your heart has ever had a key.
I can't endure any more pain,
I will let you go and please don't come back again.

The thought of your scent,
Will hunt me till the end.
The thought of your touch,
I will miss very much.

Doubts

Why are you so confused and don't let me inside your heart?
Why do we always argue and end up being apart?
Why do you hurt me so much when you know you want me in your life?
Why can you just let love flow so we could be happy just you and I?
I feel the passion in your kisses and the way you hold me tight
I feel the passion when we make love and how you want me each and every night
I see the way you look at me even when you don't notice me looking at you too
I watch every part of your body from head to toe and my heart starts beating for you
Whenever we make love and I have you in my arms
I want to touch and feel your body heat and in my mind I hear the fire alarm go off
Because our love making is hot, passionate and so intense
That's why I don't understand why we can't get it together, it just doesn't make sense
Stop fighting the love you feel for me and just let it be
Can't you see that with your doubts you could be ruining something beautiful and sweet!
Stop torturing yourself, including me with all your doubts
Doubts that I may hurt you, doubts that this won't last, why can we just try and work it out!
Let's just learn from one another because love like this has no room for doubts

11/02/09
12:21pm

Don't Walk Away

The rain will hide my tears
Tears that you will never see
Tears that slowly flow from my eyes
The day we said good bye
Standing all alone in the rain
Trying to contain myself from all this pain
But I can't do it, I love you and I can't let you go
Please come back to me, I can't take this anymore
I promise you one thing
Because you mean so much to me
That I will love you forever
And we will always be together
Please don't walk away from me
Because now I can clearly see
That you and I are meant to be!
Together always can't you see?
My darling please just stay
I don't want you to walk away
Never walk away from my life
I love you and I would love to be your wife

5/14/02

Drifting Away

I felt your love and your passion drifting away some time ago
I felt it but I refused to believe it because I didn't want to let you go
I felt it whenever you kissed my lips without the passion I once felt
That passion that used to make me feel like I was ready to melt
You stopped touching me and wrapping your arms around me during the night
That candlelight that once lit the entire room when you used to hold me tight
The wind came and blew it away the day we said goodbye
There's darkness now in my heart because you're no longer by my side
Now I'm drifting away in this dark and lonely emptiness
There's no more laughter, there's no more happiness
You took it with you when you ripped my heart from my chest
I thought you were really different from all the rest
I thought you truly loved me and that you would never hurt me
But you hurt me like no other man ever did!
You took and took till you couldn't take no more
Then you took my heart and tossed it on the floor
Like a piece of garbage that had no value anymore
Drifting away is my heart beating now that you're gone
Because I no longer have the heart I used to have before
You have now destroyed everything that used to be sweet and pure!

8/3/09

I Don't Trust You

My trust in you has faded away,
Can no longer be married to you another day.
I gave you my life and I gave you two kids,
You were lying to me in each and every kiss.

I remember all the pain that you put me through,
I wouldn't of married you if I knew you couldn't be true.
Everyone kept saying it's just an infatuation,
But you put our marriage in a stage of destruction.

I shall never trust you again,
You will never give me any more pain.
I will get a divorce and take both of my kids
For I am a good woman and I know I'll be missed

I'm Giving Up!

I don't know if this relationship is working out
I do love you, I do care about you and you're the person I can't live without
I am just not happy and I just don't feel like I am someone special in your life
I am so confused and I really don't know if this relationship is just a lie

I realize that not all the love stories are fairy tales and end up in happy endings
You work and work to make the best possible without complaining
I am just so tired of giving all of me and getting nothing in return
When is someone going to do something for me, when will it be my turn?

When will someone think of me and give me all that I want and need?
I think is time for me to say good bye and see what the world has out there for
me
It hurts so much that you were not the one and you couldn't see
How much I brought into your life and how good it could have been

I'm giving up on all the dreams I had for you and I
I'm giving up because we just don't see eye to eye
I'm giving up because you don't seem to care about us anymore!
You don't care about our future or about this broken heart that's tender and soar.

8/25/09

I Need an Answer

Something tells me there's something going on
Can you just tell me what's on your mind!
I sometimes feel like you really don't care for me
But, I keep my mouth shut because I'm afraid of you getting angry

I continue to hold things inside and I know that's not right
I just don't want to say something and have it turn into a fight
The way it always starts with us,
I am really trying not to make a fuss

I realize that we are like opposite sides of the coin
But even so, we both need to feel like we're in a place we both enjoy
I am so tired of feeling like my life has no meaning to you
I am so tired of being shut down every time I try to be there for you

I need an answer, why do you hurt me so much?
If I have never asked you for anything but your tender touch
I need an answer, are you trying to push me away?
Because if that's the case, we don't need to waste another day!

My Dream of You

I went to bed last night and you were in my dream
My dream was based on a place far away from here
Everything was perfect, and everything seemed like paradise
We were both walking hand in hand staring at the stars
Then you looked at me asked me if I would die for you
I said, you are my life, and I am soon to be your wife
Yes my love, I would do anything for you and even give you my life
I love you now and until the end of time
I love you with all my heart and soul now tell me, what's on your mind?
We came to a stop as we both looked at the moon
You said to me very softly, I don't have much time
And I must tell you I will die very soon
As my eyes started to fill up with tears, you said to me
I would also die for you my love, please don't be sad
I woke up with tears in my eyes and my heart beating fast
My first reaction was to call you and you didn't pick up
There was a chill that went through my body and it would not stop
After so many calls my telephone rings
My caller id says it's from you but it was one of your kids
There was a long pause as they began to say
I am sorry for all the calls we missed
A brief silence on the other end made me sick
Then all these thoughts of you started fading from my head
Your son says "I'm sorry to be the one to tell you but my father is dead"
A wind of your scent hit my face and dried my tears away
My dream of you came true and all the signs were there
My dream of you has taken you from my side
The image of your face will always be in my heart for as long as I am alive
Because you came to me in my dream just to say good bye…

4/9/09

Sadness in my Heart

It's sad to see the person you love from another view
It's sad to feel deep inside when they're not telling you the truth
It's sad because I gave him all of me and so much more
It's sad to feel defeated when you fought and fought till you were soar.
What can you do, when they can't see you the way you see them?
When they don't love you as much and they don't treat you like a precious gem
What can you do when you try so hard to be the person they really want?
They want to change you and tell you how to be and how to feel all the time
They're not perfect, but yet they want this perfect one.
They're confuse because in reality they really don't know what they want
They make excuses, to make you feel like you're the one at fault
It almost feels like opening up a wound and poring salt
It hurts to see how they can't be open minded and see things from a different angle
They only see what they want to see so how can you stop this battle?
The war is over and I don't want to fight this battle anymore
The sadness in my heart will have to deal with another scar.

7/5/09

To lose you Completely

There were so many things I wanted to do
There were so many things I wanted to say
What will I do now, if I don't have you?
You are gone from my future, my past and my today

You have gone to another place
Another place that it's out of my way
To another place that's really too far away
To lose you completely was something I wasn't ready to face

We had plans and now I only have memories
Memories that I could never explain to another man
Memories that soon enough will become stories
Memories that will always remain in my head

I will always wonder how it would be if you were here today
I will also wonder what would be like with you around
Would it be a life made out of clay?
Or would it be strong like a mountain sitting on the grown

Those are the questions I will always have
And now all I have is to look ahead
Erasing all the memories I have in my head
Because I am alive and you are now dead

9/8/01

Unnecessary Calls

Sometimes I feel like you call me just to say hello
Sometimes I feel like you are just a foe
Do you enjoy the pleasure of seeing me fall?
What kind of pleasure do you get from these unnecessary calls?
Playing games is all you know and I'm really tired of your crap
Next time you call, I can't guarantee I will not snap
I tried to be the kind of person you wanted me to be
But it was useless to please you and that I can clearly see
You're not the one for me, so why do continue to call me
Just erase that number you have and let me be free
Free of these unnecessary calls and free of you
You and I have nothing else to talk about, you and I are through!
Can you please just leave me alone?
I think it's time to let go and time to move on!
So stop all these unnecessary calls
It's better for all of us involved!

11/9/09
2:41pm

65

Once upon a time

There was a time when I felt like you and I were indestructible
And there was a time I felt my love for you was unconditional
But slowly someone else took that sparkle in my eye
And yet I still cared for you someone else was erasing you from my mind
That person filled the emptiness you left behind
The emptiness you created but you were too busy to notice
The problems that you tried to hide under the surface
Have suddenly taken an effect on the way I feel for you
Your attempt to make it right is now too late because I met someone new
This person holds me in his arms at night
We walk hand in hand and he raps his arms around me real tight
He makes sweet love to me till the morning light
He makes me feel like I am a part his life
Once upon a time, I wished that for you and I
Once upon a time, I wanted to be your wife
Now all of that has changed because you never took the time
The time to really get to know how much love I felt for you
The time to really understand how many nights I cried for you
And now all of that has to come to an end because I found it in someone new

01/14/10

Three Women and One Man

How do you deal with all the pain?
When there are three women and just one man
He tells each and every one of us that you're his woman
Keeping secrets from all of us, has become his perfection
Lying bastard! His love turned out to be Deception
He took all our money and crushed our hearts
And all along he played it smart!
He played us all for a damn fool!
All along telling each of us "I love you"
"I'm a good man, I will never hurt you"
"There's no one else in my life except for you"
"You are my rock and can't live without you"
Lies and more lies he said to us time and time again!
He ran over our hearts with a goddamn train
But karma is a bitch and he will get his fair share
He may be paying for it now and that's why he can't get ahead
He's unemployed, losing his house and totally broke
He's getting what he deserves, that's why he can't find work
But you messed with the wrong women, because we'll see you in court!

03/9/2011
By: Liz Maldonado

Lies

Yesterday you were my world
Today you don't exist to me anymore
All the lies you said to me, you were saying it in someone else's bed
You sounded so honest but I guess it was all an act
To have believed all the lies you said to me over and over again
I must of really been in sane!
Lying, cheating, bastard!
This game you came to mastered!
How could you really sleep at night?
How will I ever erase your evil soul from mind!
I wish I had this magical button and press rewind!
Back to where you didn't exist in my life!
I wished that this was just another one of those bad dreams
Instead I'm dealing with all of your goddamn schemes
Why didn't I listen to my intuition?
Why did you become my addiction?
You are a sorry excuse of a man without decency
With no scruples, no shame and no honesty
But one day you will face your evil twin
And you will remember all the women you hurt way back when!
Lies & Lies that you said to me over and over again
Thank God I saw your true colors and brought this to an end!

3/18/11

Dreams and Fantasies

I once had a dream that my life was complete
I dreamed that I had found a man wonderful and sweet
I would lay down at night and he was there waiting for me
To hold me in his arms as we both went to sleep
I woke up in the middle of the night filled with joy
But realized that it was just a dream that you slowly destroyed
You would speak to me about marriage and our future together
You fed me all these lies that soon turn into cancer
For months and months I fantasized to spend the rest of my life with you
And in the back of your mind you knew that would never come true
You took advantage of my feelings and you didn't care about breaking my heart
You used me as a target and you didn't care where you through the dart
How will I ever heal from all this pain I'm feeling?
How can I tell my heart to keep on beating?
How can I tell my soul to keep on living?
When will I ever learn to love again if I stopped caring!
Dreams and Fantasies are just a waste of time
Dreams and Fantasies are illusions created in your mind
I stopped believing in dreams and fantasies because of you
And now I must go on with my life with a different view!

Miscellaneous Poems

The Wolf

Confusion and distractions come in all forms
Is like chasing the rainbow after the storm
You could never quite understand the reason why
You can stand on your tippy toes and still can't touch the sky
Understanding a man is also very hard
That's one of the reasons why you have to be on guard
To be able to tell the ones who are in disguise
The wolf in sheep clothing is not very apparent to the eye
Men disguise themselves as sheep to get their prey
And after they have you they take the disguise away
They turn into wolves but they are also the best lovers
Once you've been with a wolf it's very hard to recover
Because they hunt every part of your body leaving nothing untouched
They are the masters in control to every single touch
They are playful but it's dangerous to get too attached
Just remember they are wolves and a wolf with a sheep is not a good match!
There's only one way, the sheep could truly be save from the wolf's bite
And that is to catch him, care for him and love him with all your might.

03.24.10

Homeless

Invisible to everyone on the street,
I'd do anything just to get something to eat.
People pass me by, always look away,
They don't realize that I haven't eaten in three days.

I'm sorry that I'm dirty, I'm sorry that I smell,
I just haven't been lucky and my health isn't well.
I don't drink, I don't smoke and never taken drugs
I don't know why people look at me afraid of being mugged.

I look ugly, but I'm not mean,
Being homeless was not a choice for me.
All I wish for is that one day this nightmare could turn into a dream,
I honestly can't tell you how I came to this extreme.

Looking into garbage cans every morning on the street,
I'm all crabby because I have nothing good to eat.
And if tomorrow you pretend not to stare,
Don't walk away just acknowledge that I'm there.

Daddy's little Girl

I watch you when you sleep
And my heart often skips a beat
Just knowing how much I love you
And always know that I would never leave you
You are my little girl, my world, my sunshine
You are everything to me and it's something I can't denied
I will be there for you whenever you need me
I will be there even when we will not agree
I know there will come a time when you will get older
But I want you to know you can rely on my shoulder
For you to put your arms around and even to cry when you're sad
Because my purpose in life is to be a good Dad
I want you to know that you fill my life with joy and everlasting happiness
Without you I would have nothing but loneliness and emptiness
You are my little girl, you are so divine, you are one of a kind
Like each star in the sky that depend on the sun to shine
I will be the sun for you and you can depend on me my dear
Because you're Daddy's little girl and I will always be here.

9/8/09

Devoted Father

I see my father from up above
I see my father so full of love
I see the way he's devoted to his kids
And from up above I'm sending you a kiss

Daddy please don't be sad for me anymore
I am up in heaven full of your love and so much more
I watch you every single day and night
I love you still even if I am out of your sight.

Be happy that I am here with God
Be happy because you have made me proud
Be happy because I will suffer no more
Be happy because I am with my savior

Devoted Father you will always be to me
Devoted Father that's all I see
Devoted Father I can still feel your touch
Devoted Father I love you so very much

12/23/08

Domestic Abuse

I can't stand another night,
Of all the arguments and fights.
I don't know how much more I can take,
I have to end this marriage for my child's sake.

My family will soon understand,
That this abuse has to come to an end.
I tried so hard to make this marriage work,
Tomorrow he'll be sorry when I walk out that door.

My son no longer has love for his father,
But he knows he can always count on his mother.
To be there for him through thick and thin,
Even when his natural father it's not there for him.

There comes a time to forgive and forget,
And the only thing that I do not regret.
Was the unconditional love I feel for my child
That gave me the strength to tolerate him for a while.

Faith in my Light

Walking alone on a dark misty night
Blinded by a single lonely bright light
Guided and keeping myself focused at that beautiful sight
At times I feel miss-guided but I still hold on t it with all my might

Never looking back at what happened in the past
Keeping my eyes forward to the light in the mist
This light has never shined as bright as this
It feels like being caressed with a tender kiss

People tend to get lost and lose their faith
But the light will always guide us, protect us and show us the way
Listen to your heart and the light will bring you to the next day
For the light is only asking that you always remember to say a little prayer.

Love for a Child

The minute you came into my life
All you knew how to do was smile and cry.
I held you tight in my arms,
So that no one could ever do any harm.

Your little tiny hands and feet,
I held your bottle for a while so you could eat.
My darling angel please don't cry,
Everything will be all right.

The love of a child is a precious one,
Child of mine, you will never be alone.
Mom will always be here to hold your hand,
Even on the times that you are bad.

So think of me when I'm old and grey,
And remember all the things I've done for you and said.
For you will grow to be a fine adult,
And if you fail in life, it will not be your fault.

My Best Friend

You have been there for me when I have been in and out of relationships
You have listened to me and you have also given me tips
You have made me see things about myself that I could never see
You are my best friend even when we didn't agree
I love you for the kind of person you are to me
I love you because I know you could never judge me
You have been the best friend anyone could ever have
You have brought my spirit up even when I have been sad
Being in your arms at night have also been part of your job
And for that I thank you from the bottom of my heart
I have also wished I could find a man just like you
But deep down I feel like that will never come true
We were born it two different time zones and that's just not fair
Because like you said "we would've been a great pair"
I am very glad I met you and that you also became my best friend
I could never thank you enough for always, always being there
We have fun, laugh and seem to get along all the time
Even with our age difference we seem to be two of a kind
The silly and inner child in us we never seem to mind
But one thing you have to stop doing and that is grabbing my thigh!

6/1/09

Hurting for You

I feel the desperation in your voice
I hear all your thoughts even through all the noise
I feel your pain and I can't help but to hurt for you
Wondering what else I can do to help you get through
It hurts so much to see you go through all this
Because you try so hard to be a good man
You are a wonderful catch and I know you try your best
You are so different from all the rest!
I am hurting for you and wish I could do more
I am hurting for you and this feeling is hard to ignore
Because everything that you go through, I feel the same
And I wish I could take all of your pain
This should not be happening to you
Please tell me what else I can do!
I feel helpless and I want you to be happy
Why is this woman making your life so crappy?
Why can she see all that she has done!
Doesn't she realize that you are the one?
I don't care how much drama she has in her life
What she has done to your heart is stab you with a knife
I will be there for you till the end
I will be by your side and the one person you can depend
I will be there to hold your hand
Because you will always be my best friend

6/26/2009
3:33pm

The Innocent Ones

You have taken the innocence from their eyes,
Their laughter is gone all you hear is the cries.
A cry for help, which nobody knows or hears,
There's a fog in their eyes, life for them will never be clear.

Afraid of going to sleep at night,
Wanting to disappear from everyone's sight!
As they grow older, their trust and anger grows stronger,
The sparkle in their eyes you once saw, you will see no longer

You have killed everything good and pure,
And for them there will never be a cure.
The innocent child has forgotten how to smile,
Looking forward to the future is no longer worthwhile.

There's no greater sin than the sex abuse,
And for you, there will never be an excuse.
For you have slowly killed the child,
And you have only created someone wild.

Appearances

Sometimes is not relevant of what it appears to be
Sometimes is just the nature of what you feel or see
Never mind what you intended to do and how far you get
All that matter is what you come to regret
Appearances could be deceiving is true!
But you can control that by not acting the fool
Don't do on to others, what you don't want done to you
Otherwise this will blow up in your face before you know
I know one cannot control the other person's emotions
And all it takes is one spark to cause that reaction
That's why is better to have some decency and respect
So that the other person doesn't start to suspect
Don't kill the trust of the person who loves you and cares for you
Because life is a full circle and it will be done to you too!
Sometimes we don't cherish what we already have in our lives
We search and search again and it never arrives
What we once had has been long gone and cannot be replaced
We find out that the appearances we made were a total waste.

Communication, Trust & Honesty!

Communication is the key to every relationship
Trust is the result of what comes out of your lips
Honesty is a reflection of your integrity
And with all these combined comes your serenity
If you don't communicate what's on your mind
You might as well walk like you're blind
No one is psychic and knows what you're thinking
Relationships are hard enough if you don't start communicating
Trust is a very simple word that means a lot
Words must match your actions and don't say, oh I forgot!
Meaning you must always say the truth even when is bad news
Because if you don't, you will find yourself singing the blues
Trust is also linked with Honesty and integrity in some way
Your life and relationship will flow easy for the rest of your days
Because if your relationship is not working out
There's just a big cloud surrounding your life with doubt
You will lose the person you love so much and the one you can't live without
By not following the simple rules of life that most people should know about!

6/30/10
4:00pm

You Make me Proud

Ever since you were young, you were just a tough little girl
You have been running around climbing trees, playing ball and in your own little world
I remember the time when you came home with a black eye
You very calm said "Mom I was just playing football with the guys!"
Do you also remember when you got run over by a kid in a bike?
You had this huge bump on your head but you didn't even cry!
Then that time in school when I dressed you up so you wouldn't look like a tomboy
It was picture day and you came home with the photo holding a mitten and a ball.
You made it through high school and now you're in college beautiful as can be
I see you now and I cannot believe my eyes, it's so hard for me to believe
This little creature that once was in my arms depending on me
With every beat of her heart jus holding on to me as tight as can be
I'm so proud of you and the kind of woman you have become
You make me proud and always remember that even when I'm not around
You are my youngest and the baby of my three kids
I love you very much with each hug and every kiss.
For my daughter Kayla

11/16/09

My Son as a Father

Seeing my son as a father is like no other
Watching him take care of his boy with no worries or bother
Since the day he was born, he was there by his side
Changing dippers, feeding him and even taking him on a ride
I love watching my son take care of his little boy
I love watching them both playing with all the toys
Teaching his son from right and wrong is not a game
Teaching him to be a real man is nothing to be ashamed
My son tries to set a good example to his son
Teaching him other things will not stop by just how to hold a crayon
I love to see my son spending time with my grandson
I have to admit that they're both very handsome
My son struggles but he just doesn't give up
Because he knows he has a son he would like to see grow up
Grow up to be a good father just like my son did with him
And teach his own son from the moment he's born till he becomes a man.
For my Son Steven

6/21/09

After all

You were the hardest one of all
You were the rebel and the one who knew it all
In spite of everything we been through you and I
You are my flesh and part of my life
You have been through ups and downs
But don't give up my darling angel cause I will try to be around
To help you, to give you what I can and what you need
Even at times when you and I don't agree
I love you with all my heart and soul
And while I'm here, you will never be alone
After all the pain and troubles you got into
After all the nights of wondering where you had gone to
After all the heart aches and disappointments you have given me
You're still my little girl and the oldest of the three
So find happiness for you and your little girls
Because the opportunity is out there and you can own the world
Please don't settle for anything less than what you deserve
Life can be harsh and sometimes cruel
But be careful because it could also throw you a curve.
For my daughter Desireé

03/11/08